THE TECHNOLOGY OF POWER

THE INITIATION
OF THE SON OF A
FINANCE CAPITALIST
INTO THE ARCANE
SECRETS OF
ECONOMIC AND
POLITICAL POWER

UNDERWORLD AMUSEMENTS

". . . the world is governed by very different personages from what is imagined by those who are not behind the scenes."
—Benjamin Disraeli
(Earl of Beaconsfield)

ISBN-13: 978-1-943687-04-6

Cover design and custom titling typeface by Paul Slagle
www.PaulSlagle.com

Edited and designed by Kevin I. Slaughter

TO MY SON

IN THIS THIN VOLUME you will find the transcripts of your initiation into the secrets of my empire. Read them again not for the arcane knowledge which is now second nature you, but in order to re-experience the shock and awe you felt twenty years ago when at age thirty the fabulous scope of my power was revealed to you by my trusted, and now mostly departed advisors. Remember the surprise, to the point of disbelief, with which you beheld the invisibly delicate, but invincible chains of deceit, confusion, and coercion with which we finance capitalists enslave this chaotic world. Remember the feats of will and strategy that have been required to retain our position. Then, inspect your retinue carefully. Your heir must be equal to and eager for the task much as you were. Choose him carefully. As I lie here waiting for the end I can afford to relish the thought our empire lasting forever as I never dared while in charge. Rational power calculations, so easily disrupted by the thrill of power, are now entirely in your hands.

"KNOW!—WILL—DARE—AND BE SILENT!"
—ALEISTER CROWLEY

THE TRANSCRIPTS

"Man is a rope stretched between the animal and the Superman a rope over an abyss."

"I teach you the Superman. Man is something to be surpassed."
—Friedrich Nietzsche

"Self reverence, self-knowledge, self-control these three alone lead to sovereign power."

—Alfred Lord Tennyson

"And nothing, not God, is greater to one than one's self is."
—Walt Whitman

"Do what thou wilt shall be the whole of the Law."
—Aleister Crowley *The Book of the Law*

MY INTRODUCTION TO YOUR INITIATION

MY SON, the time has arrived to make formal what you have confidently awaited for some years. Of all your brothers, sisters, and cousins, as well as the offspring of my close allies, I have chosen you to be heir to my empire. All the trust funds, foundations, and accounts through which my empire is controlled shall pass into your hands upon my retirement. All my alliances, understandings, and enmities with my handful of peers around the globe shall gradually become yours. Over the next twenty years we shall collaborate closer and closer, you and I, until, we finally act as one.

For ten years you have toured my empire in a succession of managerial assignments and are now familiar with the outward operations of my crucial banking, foundation, governmental, and think tank organizations. Until now, my advisors and I have deflected your questions as to how and if my diverse operations and holdings, which seem autonomous and even contradictory, are integrated into an organic whole to serve the dynasty's interests. The fact that you asked these questions, rejecting my carefully nurtured public image as an idle, coupon clipping philanthropist, was a major factor in the high esteem in which I hold you. Most of your competitors found puppet leadership in any one of my organizations so awesome and gratifying that they immediately eliminated themselves from the contest for the top position which you have won. Such men of limited vision are necessary for my success. They bend unconsciously to the subtle pressures to which I expose them. They can be led in any direction I choose by simple-minded rationalizations aimed at their vanity without being privy to my motives which would be short lived secrets in their undisciplined and envious minds .

Most important in your selection as my successor, however was your psychological nature which has been faithfully reported to me over the years by my associates, many of whom have advanced psychological training. A man in my position must have total mastery over his emotions. All actions affecting the power of the dynasty must be taken on the basis of coldly reasoned power calculations if the dynasty is to survive and prosper at the expense of its subjects and rivals. All power is impossible to those whose pursuit is ruled by sentimentality, love, envy, power-lust, revenge, prejudice, hatred, justice, alcohol, drugs, or sexual desire. Sustained power is impossible to those who repress all their irrational longings into their subconscious only to have them return in compulsive, out of control behavior that inevitably leads to their ruin. Although often clothed in the rationalizations of power calculation, compulsive behavior is at root, the emotionalism of a frightened child, desperately projecting his inner agony into a reality he is afraid to understand, much less master.

Although you now must begin to pursue it consciously you have already displayed the alienation from your emotional nature that is so essential to achieving real worldly power. You must recognize your emotional nature as a primitive survival mechanism that was appropriate for the jungle and perhaps useful to common men, but useless for the tasks that confront us finance capitalists. Attachment to what you do, just because you do it, is the primary psychological characteristic of ordinary mortals. Such cognitive dissonance spells disaster for us. Our emotional mechanism makes our lives worth living, but is no guide to the occult arts of intrigue. So, continue to gratify your senses and emotions fully at your leisure. As long as the empire prospers you will have the resources to indulge in systematic gratification which will leave your irrational urges sated and, therefore, powerless. You will never be in the unenviable position of the middle class strivers who must, from lack of resources, repress their emotional natures if they are to attain any power whatever during their lives. Typically, they end up taking their pleasure from the victories and cruelties of their struggle. Thus, their end ceases to be power and they eventually defeat themselves with reckless behavior in pursuit of dominant thrills.

I have brought you into seclusion with my most trusted advisors in order to inaugurate a new phase of your instruction. Your formal training in the "official" political-economic world is now complete. This weekend will mark the beginning of your training in the occult technology of power that lurks behind outer appearances. As your tutors will explain, "occult" or secret knowledge is the basis of all power in human society, so I use the word "occult" advisedly, in its pristine usage. As I am sure you are aware by now, productivity in itself does not secure power and therefore does not secure the gratifications of life. After all, slaves can be productive. None of my organizations in which you served so well are concerned with advancing the techniques of satisfying human needs and desires. Rather, all are dedicated to the surreptitious centralization of productive, but especially coercive, efforts in my hands or in creating the intellectual climate in which such veiled control would be tolerated in the future. I destroy or paralyze productive efforts that cannot be ensnarled in my web

After a break Professor A. will take the floor in order to put finance capitalism into full biological perspective. His short talk will be followed by similar abbreviated summaries by his six associates, all of whom you know well. The rest of the weekend will be devoted to forthright fielding of your questions.

1

"Are we not all predatory animals by instinct? If humans ceased wholly from preying upon each other, could they continue to exist?"

—Anton Szandor LaVey

"Nature, to be commanded must be obeyed."

—Francis Bacon

PROFESSOR A.
ON THE ROLE OF
FRAUD IN NATURE

Organisms typically base their success primarily on deception and rely on actual force or mutually advantageous trade (symbiosis) as little as possible. This should be nearly self-evident, but is generally overlooked due to the moral codes we elitists foist on our subjects. Let me give a few examples in case the moral culture has to some extent impaired your powers of objective observation. Camouflage is universal among predators and victims alike. Blossoms imitate fragrances and colors which are sexually attractive to certain insects in order to effect pollination. Dogs bark ferociously and feign attack on enemies of whom they are, in fact, terrified. The Venus Fly Trap plant lures flies to their deaths. Men proclaim their altruism to others and even themselves while they selfishly scramble for personal advantage. If you doubt that fraud is normal in nature you should read section three of the first chapter of Robert Ardrey's, *The Social Contract* for a wealth of fascinating examples.[1]

Human mental prowess and communicative powers have merely provided superb elaboration on nature's old theme of fraud and added its own distinctive feature: self delusion. Primitive animal hierarchies are based on bluff and bluster, and each member is well aware of and accepts, at least temporarily, its position in the hierarchy. The same wild enthusiasm and fascination for dominance and submission rages in human hearts. However, fraud is taken one step further. Not only is fraudulent bluff and bluster

---

1   Of course Ardrey fails to grasp the full application to contemporary human society of his brilliant insights into man's animal nature.

used to achieve dominance but fraudulent altruism and collective institutions are used to conceal dominance once achieved. Human hierarchies, in contrast to the animal variety, are best sustained when the members are deluded regarding the oppressive nature, or better, even the very existence of the hierarchy!

Visible rulers are highly vulnerable. Thus we see visible rulers claiming to be representatives of God, the common good, the material forces of history, the general will (either through vote or intuition), tradition, or other intellectual "spooks" that serve to lessen the envy of the ruled for the rulers. Encouraging such self delusions among the masses of the ruled is universal for visible governments. However, such spooks are little protection for the leaders of such systems against their sophisticated elite rivals and no protection against men like your father. The Roman Empire was unquestioned by the mass of its subjects for centuries, but the Emperors lived in constant fear of coup and assassination.

By embracing deception wholeheartedly at every level, finance capitalism, or rule through money, has fashioned the ultimate system yet devised for the secure exercise of power. Men like your father, the hidden masters of finance capitalism, govern those who govern, produce, and think through invisible financial tentacles, the operations of which will be elucidated later by my colleagues. Dominance in all aspects of society is surreptitiously accomplished while the great majority of the ruled, and even most of the visible leaders, believe themselves to be fairly autonomous, if harried, members of a pluralistic society. Nearly everyone believes major decisions to be the vector sum of autonomous pressures exerted by business, labor, government, consumers, social classes, and other special interests. In fact, the vectors of societal power are carefully balanced by us so that any net movement is in a direction chosen by us. The only fly in the ointment is the occasional, but extremely messy, interferences by competing financial dynasties. This disconcerting problem will not be a major topic for this weekend.

I now yield to Professor Q. who will elucidate the central secrets of your father's immense money power.

2

"The theory of aggregate production which is the point of the following book, nevertheless can be much easier adapted to the conditions of a totalitarian state than the theory of production and distribution of a given production put forth under conditions of free competition. . ."

—John Maynard Keynes
Forward to the German
Edition of the
General Theory
September 7, 1936

PROFESSOR Q.
ON OCCULT KNOWL-EDGE AS THE KEY TO POWER

Throughout history, secure ruling elites arise through secret, or occult knowledge which they carefully guard and with-hold from outsiders The power of such elites or cults dimin-ishes as their occult knowledge is transformed into "scientific" knowledge and vanishes as soon as it becomes "common sense." Before analyzing the secrets of the finance capitalist money cult let us glance for historical perspective at occult astronomy, the oldest source of stable rule known to man of which astrology is but the pathetic remnant. As soon as men abandoned the life of wandering tribal hunters to till the soil, they needed to predict the seasons. Such knowledge was required in order to know when to plant, when to ex-pect floods in fertile valleys, when to expect rainy seasons, and so on. Months of back breaking work were wasted by the unavailability of the calendar, a convenience we take for granted. The men who first studied and grasped the regu-larities of sun, moon, and stars that presage the seasons had a valuable commodity to sell and they milked it to the fullest at the expense of their credulous fellow men. The occult priest-hoods of early astronomers and mathematicians such as the designers of Stonehenge, convinced their subjects that they alone had contact with the gods, and thus, they alone could assure the return of planting seasons and weather favorable to bountiful harvests. The staging (predicting) of solar and lunar eclipses was particularly effective in awing the commu-nity The general success resulting from following the priest-hood's tilling, planting, nurturing, and harvesting time tables insured the priesthood's power. Today's Christmas holiday season continues the tradition set by ancient priesthoods, who conducted rituals on the winter solstice to reverse the retreat of the sun from the sky. Their invariable success was followed by wild celebrations. Popular knowledge of seasonal regularities was discouraged by every manner of mysticism and outlandish ritual imaginable. Failures in prediction were blamed on sins of the people and used to justify intensified oppression. For centuries people who had literally no idea of the number of days between seasons and couldn't count anyway, cheerfully gave up a portion of their harvests, as well as their most beautiful daughters, to their "faithful servants" in the priesthoods .

The power of our finance capitalist money cult rests on a similar secret knowledge, primarily in the field of economics. Our power is weakened by real advances in economic science.[2] However, we established money lords have been able to prolong and even reverse our decline by systematically corrupting economic science with fallacious and spurious doctrines. Through our power in the universities, publishing, and mass media we have been able to reward the sincere, professorial cranks whose spurious doctrines happen to rationalize in terms of "common good" the government supported institutions, laws, and economic measures upon which our money powers depend. Keynesianism is the highest form of phoney economics yet developed to our benefit. The highly centralized, mixed economy resulting from the policies advocated by Lord Keynes for promoting "prosperity" has all the characteristics required to make our rule invulnerable to our twin nemeses: real private competition in the economic arena and real democratic process in the political arena. *Laissez-faire* or free market, classical economics was our original attempt to corrupt economic science. Its beautiful internal consistency blinded economists for many years to the fact that it had virtually nothing to do with current reality. However, we are so powerful today that it is no longer possible

---

2   Fortunately, the public at large and most revolutionaries remain totally ignorant of economics.

to conceal our imposing institutions with the appearances of free competition. Keynesianism rationalizes this omnipotent state which we require, while retaining the privileges of private property on which our power ultimately rests. Although the interim reforms advocated by Marx in his *Communist Manifesto,* such as central banking, income tax, and other centralizing measures, can be corrupted to coincide exactly with our requirements, we no longer allow Marxist movements major power in developed countries. Our coercive in institutions are already in place. Any real steps toward communism would mean our downfall. Of course, phoney Marxism is an excellent ideological veil in which to cloak our puppet dictators in underdeveloped areas.

Secondarily, the power of the lords of money rests on an occult knowledge in the area of politics and history. We have quite successfully corrupted these sciences. Although many people are familiar with our secrets through such books as *1984* by the disillusioned George Orwell, few take them seriously and usually dismiss such ideas as paranoia. Since real politics is motivated by individual self-interest, history is viewed most accurately as a struggle for power and wealth. We do our best to obscure this self-evident truth by popularizing the theory that history is made by the impersonal struggles between ideas, political systems, ideologies, races, and classes. Through systematic infiltration of all major intellectual, political, and ideological organizations, using the lure of financial support and instant publicity, we have been able to set the limits of public debate within the ideological requirements of our money power

The so-called Left-Right political spectrum is our creation. In fact, it accurately reflects our careful, artificial polarization of the population on phoney issues that prevents the issue of our power from arising in their minds. The Left supports civil liberties and opposes economic or entrepreneural liberty. The Right supports economic liberty and opposes civil liberty. Of course neither can exist fully (which is our goal) without the other. We control the Right-Left conflict such that both forms of liberty are suppressed to the degree we require Our own liberty rests not on legal or moral "rights," but on our control of the government bureaucracy and courts which apply the complex, subjective regulations we dupe the public into supporting for our benefit .

Innumerable meaningless conflicts to divert the attention of the public from our operations find fertile ground in the bitter hatreds of the Right-Left imbroglio. Right and Left are irreconcilable on racial policy, treatment of criminals, law enforcement, pornography, foreign policy, women's lib, and censorship to name just a few issues. Although censorship in the name of "fairness" has been useful in broadcasting and may yet be required in journalism, we generally do not take sides in these issues. Instead we attempt to prolong the conflicts by supporting both sides as required. War, of course, is the ultimate diversionary conflict and the health of our system. War provides the perfect cover of emergency and crisis behind which we consolidate our power. Since nuclear war presents dangers even to us, more and more we have resorted to economic crisis, energy shortages, ecological hysteria, and managed political drama to fill the gap. Meaningless, brush-fire wars, though, remain useful.

We promote phoney free enterprise on the Right and phoney democratic socialism on the Left. Thus, we obtain a "free enterprise" whose "competition" is carefully regulated by the bureaucracy we control and whose nationalized enterprises are controlled directly through our government. In this way we maintain a society in which the basis of our power, legal titles to property and money, remain secure, but in which the peril of free, unregulated competition is avoided and popular sovereignty is nullified. The democratic process is a sitting duck for our money power. Invariably we determine the candidates of the major parties and then proceed to pick the winners. Any attempts at campaign reforms simply put the rules of the game more firmly under our government's control.

Totalitarianism of the fascist or communist varieties is

no danger to us as long as bastions of private property remain to serve as our bases of operation. Totalitarian governments of both Right and Left, because of the vulnerability of their highly visible leaders to party rivals, can be manipulated easily from abroad. Primarily, totalitarian dictatorships efficiently prevent new money lords that could challenge our power from arising in whole continents, civilizations, and races.

Perhaps a few words on ideology proper are in order before I conclude. The only valid ideology, of course is rational egoism, that is, the maximization of the individual's gratification by whatever means prove practical. This requires power over nature, especially, when possible, power over other humans who are the most versatile and valuable tools of all. Fortunately, we do not have a society of egoists. Money lords would be impossible in such a society as the mental spooks and rationalizations by which we characteristically manipulate and deceive would be a laughing stock Under such circumstances a policy of live and let live or true "*laissez-faire*" anarchy might be the only alternative. Certainly a hierarchical order would be difficult to maintain by force alone. However, in the current era, while minds are yet in the thrall of altruistic collectivistic, and divine moralistic spooks, the egoist's rational course is to utilize such spooks to control others.

The next speaker, Professor M., will detail the key institution of our power: Central Banking.

3

"It (a bank) can take the depositors' goods, the goods that it holds for safekeeping, and lend them out to people on the market. It can earn interest on these loans, and as long as only a small percentage of depositors ask to redeem their certificates at any one time, no one vs the wiser. Or, alternatively, it can issue pseudo warehouse receipts for goods that are not there and lend these on the market. this is the more subtle practice. the pseudo receipts will be exchanged on the same basis as the true receipts, since there is no indication on their face whether they are legitimate or not.

It should be clear that this practice is outright fraud."

—Murray Rothbard
Man, Economy, and State

"The bold effort the present bank has made to control the Government, the distress it has wantonly produced. . . are but premonitions of the fate that awaits the American People should they be deluded into a perpetuation of this institution (The Bank of the United States), or the establishment of another like it."

—Andrew Jackson
December 2, 1834

PROFESSOR M.
ON THE ECONOMICS OF CENTRAL BANKING

As you have a doctorate degree in economics from a great university I will touch as lightly as my verbosity allows on facts accepted by economic "science" and proceed to occult aspects of Central Banking. Since the division of labor is the key to all human achievement and satisfaction, a system of exchange is crucial. Barter is hopelessly complicated. A command economy, in which each does and receives what he is told, is also hopelessly cumbersome and fails to take advantage of individual initiative, ability, and concrete knowledge. A medium of exchange, money, is the obvious solution.[3]

When left to themselves people of a given geographical area settled upon a durable luxury commodity, usually gold or silver, to use as money. Because money is a store of value as well as a medium of exchange, people saved part of their gold income rather than spending it all. This gold was often stored in the vaults of a local goldsmith, the precursor of the modern banker, for safe keeping. The depositor received a receipt that entitled him to an equal quantity and quality of gold on demand from the goldsmith. At some point the goldsmith realized that there was no reason he could not loan out some of the gold for interest as long as he kept gold on hand sufficient to meet the fairly predictable withdrawal rate. After all, he simply promised to pay on demand, not bold the gold as such. Better yet, he could simply issue more receipts for gold than he bad gold and the receipts, renamed notes, could circulate freely among the populace as money. However, he soon found that there was a definite limit set

---

3   Even our highly centralized economies on the socialist model now enthusiastically embrace money as an indispensable simplifying tool in their economic planning.

on this process by reality. Not all the extra notes issued circulated forever among the public. The rate of note redemption began to increase rapidly as the receipts passed into the hands of people unfamiliar with his reputation and especially when competitive goldsmiths, always eager for more gold reserves, came into possession of his notes. To prevent a disastrous run on his gold reserves, note issuance had to be kept within bounds. But the spending power of over-issuance was a grave temptation. Especially relished was the power over governments, industry, and merchants that the miraculous loan power of the goldsmith could obtain. Many succumbed to temptation, overextended themselves and brought ruin to their depositors while others slowly became wealthy bankers by pursuing conservative loan policies.

At this point, according to economic "science," Central Banks are instituted to protect the public from periodic financial catastrophe at the hands of unscrupulous fractional reserve bankers. Nothing could be further from the truth. Central Banks are established to remove the limitation on over issuance that reality places on competitive banking systems. As early as ancient Babylon and India, Central Banking, the art of monopolizing the issuance of money, had been developed into a perfect method for looting the general public. Even today many bankers copy the traditions of the earlier exploitive priesthoods and design their banks to resemble temples! Defenses of Central Banking are simply part of the deception that lies at the heart of all power elites.

Let us look at the way a new Central Bank is created where none has existed previously. We bankers approach the Prince or ruling assembly[4] with a compelling proposal: "Grant our bank a national Charter to regulate private banking and to issue legal tender notes, that is, force our notes to be accepted as payment for all debts, pubic and private. In exchange we will provide the government all the notes it

---

4   Both of whom always want more money to fight wars or to curry favor with the people and, typically, are ignorant of economics.

prudently requires at interest rates easily payable with existing taxes. The increased government purchasing power thus created will simultaneously assure the power an prestige of the currently precarious nation and stimulate the sluggish, credit starved economy to new heights of prosperity. Most important the violent banking panics and credit collapses caused by unscrupulous private bankers will be replaced by our even handed, beneficent and scientific management of money and banking. Our public spirited expertise will be at the disposal of the state while we remain independent enough of momentary political pressures to assure sound management."

For a while this system seems to work remarkably well with full employment for everyone. The government and public does not notice that we issuers of the new notes are using the notes we create out of thin air to surreptitiously build economic empires at the expense of established interests. Because of the legal tender laws, few of the new notes issued by the Central Bank are returned for redemption in gold. In fact, private banks and even a few foreign banks may begin to use the Central Bank's notes as reserves for further issuance of credit. Soon enough, though, prices begin to rise as the added notes increase demand relative to the quantity of goods and services. As the value of their savings decline more and more foreigners in particular begin to question the value of the Central Bank's notes and start to demand redemption in gold. We, of course, do not take responsibility for the rampant inflation when it comes. We blame inflation on evil speculators who drive up prices for personal gain, as well as the greed of organized labor and business who are promptly made subject to wage and price controls. Even the consumer can be made to feel guilty for agreeing to pay the high prices! Mistaking symptoms for causes the government accepts the banker's analysis of the problem and continues to give the Bank free reign in monetary policy.

By slowing the rate of note issuance periodically, the ultimate crisis stage is postponed until many decades after the original Central Bank Charter was granted. Before the rapidly dwindling gold reserves on which faith in our Bank depends is exhausted we abruptly contract our loan volume to private industry and government as well. With the contraction of the money supply a great deflationary crash begins in earnest with all its attendant unemployment, bankruptcies, and civil strife. We do not take responsibility for the depression. We blame it on evil hoarders who are refusing to spend their money and the prophets of doom who are spoiling business confidence. The government accepts this analysis and leaves monetary policy in our hands. If things go well we bankers channel the fury and unrest into puppet movements and pressure groups that carry our agents into full control of the government. Once in charge we devalue our outstanding bank notes in terms of gold and make them inconvertible for all but possibly foreign Central Banks and begin plans to restore a "prosperity" that will be totally ours.

When lucky, we are able to confiscate the gold of private citizens as punishment for hoarding during the climax of the depression.

Once the old order is subdued during the chaos of the crash and desperation of the depression, the field is open for our full finance capitalist system to be realized. If the money lords behind the Central Bank can avoid lapsing into political and economic competition among themselves a new and lasting order can be established. A war timed for this period of consolidation provides the perfect excuse for the regimentation required to crush all opposition.

Professor B., a former Chairman of a Central Bank, will explain the functioning of the Central Plank in the typical, fully developed finance capitalist system.

4

"We are undone, my dear sir, if legislation is still permitted which makes our money, much or little, real or imaginary, as the moneyed interests shall choose to make it."

—Thomas Jefferson

"From now on depressions will be scientifically created."

—Congressman Charles A. Lindberg, Sr., 1923

PROFESSOR B.
ON THE FUNCTION OF THE CENTRAL BANK IN THE MATURE FINANCE CAPITALIST SYSTEM

In its pristine form a Central Bank is a private monopoly of a nation's money and credit issuance supported by the coercive power of the state. That the Central Bank be directly in our hands is vital until our new order is firmly established throughout the governmental, business, intellectual and political spheres of society. After our order is consolidated, formal nationalization of the Central Bank with great fanfare is usually advisable in order to dispel any lingering suspicion that it is operated for private gain. Of course only loyal agents of the dynasty are allowed to obtain high offices in the Bank and our power remains intact. Obvious private monopolies are always the targets of sharp reformist agitators. Only the most paranoid, however, can see through the public facade to the private monopoly of the nationalized or quasi-nationalized Central Bank.

The Central Bank is the primary monopoly on which all our monopoly power depends. The occult power of the Central Bank to create money out of nothing is the fountainhead that fuels our far flung financial and political empire. I will make a quick survey of a few of the ways this secret money power is brought to bear.

Basically, the power of our Central Bank flows from its control over the points of entry into the economy of new inflationary money which it creates out of thin air. Ordinarily, bills of exchange, acceptances, private bonds, government bonds and other credit instruments are purchased by the Central Bank through specially privileged dealers in order to put the new money, often only checking accounting entries, into circulation. The dealers are allowed a large profit since they are fronts operated by our agents. Our purchase of government securities pleases the government, as our purchase of private debt pleases private debtors. As a quid pro quo to assure "good management" our agents are given directorships, managerial posts, and offices in the corporations and government's so benefitted. As the addiction to the narcotic of inflationary easy credit grows and grows we demand more and more control of our dependent entourage of governments and corporations. When we finally end the easy credit to "combat inflation" the enterprises and governments either fall directly into our hands, bankrupt, or are rescued at the price of total control.

Also, we ruling bankers control the flow of money in the economy through the wide authority of the Central Bank to license, audit, and regulate private banks. Banks that loan to interests outside the loyal entourage are "audited" by the Central Bank and found to be dangerously overextended. Just a hint of insolvency from the respected Central Bank authorities is enough to cause a run on the disobedient bank or at least dry up its vital lines of credit. Soon the banking establishment learns to follow the hints and nods of your father's agents at the Central Bank automatically.

Further, the periodic cycles of easy money and tight money that we initiate through our control of the Central Bank cause corresponding fluctuations in all markets. Our inner circle knows in advance the timing of these cycles and, therefore reaps windfall profits by speculating in commodity, stock, currency, gold, and bond markets. Monopolistic stock and commodity Exchanges are a vital adjunct to our power made possible by our Central Bank power. We do not allow a fair auction market to exist, but make a great show of "tough" government regulation to create a false sense of confidence among small investors. With the aid of our regulatory charade and financial power we are able to maintain Exchanges tailored to our entourage's need to manipulate stock prices at the expense of independent investors. Our privileged specialists on the floors of our Exchanges, aided by the propaganda of our financial press and brokerage houses, continually play on naivete and greed to drain the savings of the unwary into our coffers. The stock, commodities, and securities held in trading accounts by the Exchange and brokerage houses provides us with a clout far beyond our own actual holdings with which we can manipulate prices and win proxy fights for corporate takeovers.

Little danger to our lucrative racket exists from public spirited regulation. Our manipulations are so complex that only the most brilliant experts could comprehend them. To most economists our Exchange operations appear to be helpful efforts to "stabilize" the market. We ruling bankers, if able to keep peace among ourselves, become richer and richer as time passes without the annoyance of exerting productive effort of benefit to others.

The next speaker, Professor G. will discuss the secrets of social legislation and policy that do so much to cement our power.

5

"There is no proletarian, not even a Communist, movement, that has not operated in the interests of money, in the direction indicated by money, and for the time being permitted by money—and that without the idealists among its leaders having the slightest suspicion of the fact. "

—Oswald Spengler
Decline of the West

"Also at the (SDS) convention, men from Business International Roundtables .... tried to buy up some radicals. These are the world's leading industrialists and they convene to decide how our lives are going to go ..... We were also offered Esso (Rockefeller) money. They want us to make a lot of radical commotion so they can look more in the center as they move to the left."

—James Kunen
*The Strawberry Statement:
Notes of a College Revolutionary*

PROFESSOR G.
ON SOCIAL AND BUSINESS LEGISLATION AND POLICY

The danger to our system clearly is not that the "people" will spontaneously rise up and dispossess us. The "people" never initiate anything. All successful movements are led from the top, usually without the knowledge of the movement, by men like your father with vast resources and brilliant plans. The real danger arises in the upper-middle classes. Occasionally, these people make vast fortunes through some brilliant technological innovation in their business or through the favor of local politicians that escape our influence. Because of their ignorance of the reality of our power, however, the new rich usually fall easily into our hands. For instance, they seldom realize until too late that the dozens of loans they may owe to apparently independent banks can be called simultaneously with a mere nod from your father. Graver danger is presented by those whose enterprises are so successful as to be self-financing. Since the advent of the corporate income tax truly self-financing corporations are extremely rare. Most disquieting is when these upstarts acquire the covert or open support and advice of your father's major international antagonists. This is particularly dangerous in countries with long democratic traditions where it is difficult to make our arbitrary rulings stick.

The best solution is to enact comprehensive taxes and business regulations in the name of the common good. Such measures reduce the incidence of significant upstart competition to manageable levels. This policy, of course, strangles innovation and productivity. Reduction of the GNPs in countries under your father's control would be acceptable in the interests of secure power under the pretext of conservation, ecology, or no-growth stability except that if carried too far your father's clout vis-a-vis his international rivals would be impaired. The most difficult problem for the money lord is determining the level of social and economic freedom he dares allow for the sake of his international power. Only method is to maintain a home base of carefully monitored, relative freedom on which to base the economic and military strength required to maintain an empire of totalitarian dictatorships abroad. The following measures, however, are found necessary by nearly all money lords:

1. *Steeply Graduated Income Tax.* Income tax does not affect us because our money was accumulated before the tax was imposed and most of it is now safely protected in our network of tax exempt foundations. Foundation income and capital can legally be used to finance the bulk of our social, economic, literary, and even political propaganda. In a pinch it is easily diverted to illegal uses. Expensive "studies" required by our profitable economic operations can be legitimately financed through foundations.

To the middle classes, however. income tax makes life into an endless treadmill. Even the most productive find themselves unable to accumulate significant capital. They are forced into the clutches of our Central Bank entourage for injections of the inflationary credit which we are privileged to create out of nothing. The self-financing wealth of the legendary 19th Century robber barons and early Twentieth Century tycoons is no longer possible. Although your grand father owed his start to just those wide-open conditions, he was among the first of the super-rich to advocate the erection of the tax wall that is now in place. Please note that in democratic countries eternal vigilance is required to prevent our tax shield from being riddled with loop holes by conniving legislators, who are usually of the tax oppressed, upper-middle class origins themselves.

2. ***Business Regulation.*** When upstarts slip through our financial tentacles and tax shields, perhaps with the aid of outsiders, a second line of defense becomes vital licensing in the crucial area of broadcasting has proven particularly necessary. This makes serious upstart-led mass political challenge impossible. Harassment by bureaucrats armed with arbitrary and voluminous industrial safety regulations is a new and increasingly effective technique. Security registration requirements, "to protect the small investor," can cause fatal delays in an upstart's ability to raise capital on the stock market. Ecological considerations are easily perverted to stymie the plans of those who would upset the stability of our carefully planned system.

Anti-trust law, however, is our ultimate weapon. The handy doctrine of "pure and perfect" competition which we have fostered in our universities is ideally suited to convicting any successful competitor, at our discretion. If the competitor charges a lower price than ours he is accused of "unfair competition" aimed at driving us from the field to impair future competition. If he asks the same price as we he is open to the charge of collusion. If he charges more than us, he is obviously exploiting his "monopoly power" at the expense of the consumer. Fortunately, the rulings of our bureaucrats are so complicated that even when successfully appealed in court many years elapse before the ruling is rendered. By then our goals are often achieved through harassment.

Product quality, safety, and testing regulations are excellent methods by which we insulate our established industries from potential competition. Beside raising the costs of entry into the auto business, for instance, the cost of "safety" can be passed to the consumer along with a healthy profit mark-up.

3. ***Subsidies, Tariffs, and Foreign Aid.*** Although direct subsidies can occasionally be procured for our entourage of corporations by appealing to the masses' desire to preserve

jobs, this exploitive technique is usually too obvious. Tariffs are easily passed, but lead to retaliation against our foreign holdings. Foreign aid and soft (sure to be defaulted) government guaranteed loans, however, fill the bill perfectly under modern conditions. Foreign aid maintains our empire of foreign dictators abroad while providing guaranteed, highly profitable sales to our corporations at home base. Foreign aid should always be contingent on the purchase of goods, usually military hardware, that only our entourage of firms can provide. Few have the courage to oppose such altruistic aid to the "starving masses" of the "third world."

4. *Centralization of Power.* Real division of power between national, state, and local government is dangerous to our system. When local politicians have real autonomy, even in limited spheres, they can do much to enable upstarts to challenge our power. Our program is to bring all levels of government under our sway through such innovations as federal aid, revenue sharing, high federal taxation, and regional government.

5. *Alliance with the Lower Classes.* In order to keep our valuable regulatory machinery in place and under our control we must have the mass support of the numerous lower classes against our vigorous, but scarce middle-class rivals. The best method is to provide the lower classes with subsidies at the expense of the middle class. This creates a mutual hatred that prevents the middle class from appealing effectively to the lower classes for support. Social security, free health care, unemployment benefits, and direct welfare payments, while doing nothing for us directly, create a dependent class whose support for our critical measures can easily be made part of a package deal. Please note also that the major labor unions began with our financing and are led to this day by leaders of our choosing. No one can rise to or remain at the top of a rough and tumble union without our financial backing. In spite of their rebellious rhetoric, bought union leaders

are the source of our power over the management of firms with widely held stock. Unions are the ultimate weapon for destroying otherwise invulnerable, self-financing rivals. Further, downward flexibility of wages and prices which obtains without widespread unionization would increase the ability of the economy to survive without our aid during the economic crises we create.

Bread and circuses are as useful today as in Roman times for mobilizing the mob against our staid adversaries. Next, Professor D. will describe our education policies.

6

"In our dreams we have limitless resources and the people yield themselves with perfect docility to our molding hands. The present educational conventions fade from our minds, and unhampered by tradition, we work our good will upon a grateful and responsive rural folk . . . The task we set before ourselves is a beautiful one, to train these people as we find them to a perfectly ideal life just as they are. So we will organize our children into a little community and teach them to do in a perfect way the things their fathers and mothers are doing in an imperfect way in the home, in shop, and on the farm."

> —The objective of Rockefeller "philanthropies" stated by him and Gates in *Occasional Letter No. 1* of Rockefeller's General Education Board.

"A general state education is a mere contrivance for molding people to be exactly like one another; and as the mold in which it casts them is that which pleases the predominant power in the government- whether this be a monarch, a priesthood, an aristocracy, or the majority of the existing generation—in proportion as it is efficient and successful, it establishes a despotism over the mind, leading by natural tendency to one over the body."

> —John Stuart Mill

PROFESSOR D.
ON THE ROLE OF
PUBLIC EDUCATION

In order to maintain our system of power, the institution of universal public education is indispensable. The anarchy of private education in which any manner of dangerous ideas could be spread cannot be tolerated. Thus we make private education financially impossible to all but the few mostly the elite offspring of our financial entourage, by means of burdensome taxation and regulation. The primary purpose of public education is to inculcate the idea that our crucial institutions of coercion and monopoly were created for the public good by popular national heroes to blunt the past power of the malefactors of great wealth. Crucial is to create the impression that, although the people have been exploited in the past, today the wealthy are at the mercy of an all-powerful government which is firmly in the hands of the people or do-gooding liberals.

For those of more sophistication who reject this Pollyanna view of reality, we promote the "liberal reformer mentality" which holds that a new era of reform is on the verge of crushing forever the last vestiges of money lordism. Of course, the reforms, after taking shape as a bewildering myriad of regulatory agencies and taxes, are found to be ineffective in subordinating our power to the popular will, whereupon we stir up another era of progressive reform.

Our contrived Left-Right spectrum which our compulsory education helps to make universal is valuable in assuring that this charade does not get out of hand. The Pollyannas in the middle are neither dangerous nor useful in this endeavor. What is needed is a feeble, but persistent right-conservatism to moderate and emasculate the liberal reforms. Conservatives tend to resist all the advances in centralized, government power that we lead the liberals to see as necessary in order to totally end the "undemocratic" power of money in society. Conservatism would rather promote a "pluralism" of competing interests in which money is the medium of competition than risk the excesses of "big government." When "liberal" reforms show signs of exceeding our intentions and actually threaten to place our key institutions in the hands of the people, we can always count on the conservatives to defend our power under the illusion that they are defending the legitimate rights of "free-enterprise capitalists." On the rare occasions when conservatives call for subjecting our enterprises to *laissez-faire* competition, we can count on the dominant liberal reformers to insist on more government interference, unaware of our desire for such, in effect, self-administered regulation. The Right has such a fear of the Left's dream of democratic collectivism and the Left such a hatred for what it sees as the Right's elitist, rugged individualism that there is little danger that they will ever join forces to overturn our government-backed monopolies even though we violate the ideals of both left and right.

Centralization of control at the state, or preferably national level, assists in building the climate of opinion we require in public education. Failing to obliterate local control, other methods nearly as effective are available. Our overwhelming financial clout in the publishing industry can induce relatively uniform textbook selection. Further leverage can be created by promoting teacher colleges and teaching machines. National teacher's associations and unions are also an excellent power base from which to foster our programs of indoctrination.

With our great influence in publishing and publicity we are able to selectively popularize educational theorists whose views are incidentally beneficial, compatible, or at least not in conflict with our own goals. This way we obtain sincere, energetic activists to propagate our desires without having to reveal our motives or even existence. We do not want an educational system that produces hard-driving individuals bent on amassing great wealth and power. Therefore, we discourage education that would develop the potential powers of students to their fullest. "Liberal" education that stresses knowledge for its own sake or even sophistry and sterile mental gymnastics is of no danger to us. "Relevant," vocational, or career oriented education also poses no danger to our power. Education that prepares students to accept a cog-like existence in our military-industrial-social-welfare-regulation complex is ideal. Progressive education with its stress on "social adjustment" also produces the conformity we require of our subjects. Emphasis on competitive sports may produce a certain amount of disruptive competitiveness among the participants, but primarily has the effect of creating life-long voyeuristic spectators who will enthusiastically sublimate their competitiveness into endless hours of following college and professional sports on the boob tube. Space spectaculars and dramatic political infighting are also marvelous diversions with which to occupy the masses.

Anyone seeking social change will gravitate to the field of education. Our strategy is simple: Let only those succeed whose influence would be compatible with our power. Encourage all who would develop the passive or receptive mode of existence. Discourage all who promote the aggressive or active capacities. Build a great cult of salvation through endless education, touting it as the "democratic" path to success. Deride the frontal approach to success of the "outmoded" rugged individualist.

Before yielding the floor to Professor X., who will discuss the role of secret societies and prestigious clubs, I would like to comment on the demise of religious education as a vehicle for social control. Religion, in its time, was a remarkable weapon for inculcating subservience, altruism, and self-abnegation among our subjects. We did not give up this weapon voluntarily. Your grandfather, for one, supported the Baptist faith well after most finance capitalists had turned wholly to secular ideologies. However, a trend toward rationality in human affairs plods along inexorably quite outside the reach of our power. Only in our totalitarian dictatorships can this trend be quashed entirely. In the semi-open societies in which our money power is based, the forces of reason can only be impeded and diverted. Some have theorized that, eventually, widespread rational egoism will overturn our order. I am confident that secular faiths and just plain confusion will suffice to sustain our power for many centuries to come.

7

"Every compulsion is put upon writers to become safe, polite, obedient, and sterile. In protest, I declined election to the National Institute of Arts and Letters some years ago, and now I must decline the Pulitzer Prize. "

—Upton Sinclair

"It is useless to deny, because it is impossible to conceal, that a great part of Europe--the whole of Italy and France and a great portion of Germany, to say nothing of other countries--is covered with a network of these secret societies, just as the superficies of the earth is now being covered with rail-roads."

—Benjamin Disraeli
(Earl of Beaconsfield)
July 14, 1856

PROFESSOR X.
ON PRESTIGIOUS ASSOCIATIONS AND SECRET SOCIETIES

In preserving and protecting our grasp on nations we must exert veiled control of all major opinion molding associations and especially prestigious clubs which attract the leaders in various fields and do so much to influence the dispensing of commanding positions in government and business. Associations of the leading scholars, businessmen, writers, religionists, artists, bureaucrats, newsmen, ideologists, publishers, broadcasters, and professional men as well as special interest groups representing laborers, farmers, consumers, racial minorities, and so on must be subtly kept under the broad limits of our sway. Since membership dues and fees are never sufficient to support their ambitious activities, voluntary, non-profit organizations are easy prey for the nearly unlimited financial resources of our entourage. However, our real motive, to further our political and economic power, must not be revealed in the process. Our policies must be laboriously rationalized in terms compatible with prevalent ideologies and moralities or the material advantage of the groups involved. Leaders of such groups are remarkably quick to accept our rationalizations when financial support is extended. We engage in outright bribery only as a last resort, and then, only in extreme cases. Our long-range interests are better served by temporarily postponing a policy victory than by risking exposure of our power by attempting outright bribery. In fact, clumsy bribery and intimidation attempts are characteristic of our foolish nouveau riche opponents.

As an example, if we decide that federal rather than state chartering or licensing of corporations would further our control over the economy, we would not simply order politicians and opinion leaders to support our desires. Corporations not relishing central control would be suspicious that something was afoot and might expose our plot. Our strategy would be as follows:

1. Sacrifice one of our less competent management teams in a well-publicized corporate scandal in order to focus attention on the "widespread problem of corporate corruption under current, lax regulations."

2. Through well-funded agents, thrust into the publicity spotlight intellectuals or groups who already support federal licensing as a piecemeal step toward socialism.[5]

3. After the issue is before the public, offer to support through foundations the "objective" study of the federal licensing proposals being discussed with an eye toward proposing legislation. Often, simultaneous support for studies by disreputable, irrational groups who will oppose the proposal is useful as well. Provide no platform for well-reasoned opposition.

4. When a ground swell of support appears to be building provide the interested lobbying organizations with plenty of funds to grease the palms of politicians. The enactment of the federal licensing law thus appears as the will of society. Last ditch opposition automatically appears mean spirited, obstructionist, reactionary, and paranoid, serving only to discredit our opposition.

In our fully developed system of finance capitalist thought control and promotion control, our hierarchy of

---

5   One can find pre-existing supporters for nearly any measure with sufficient effort.

prestigious associations is capped by a single prestige society: The Council of World Affairs. This organization is a front for the secret society of which your father is head. This secret society is made up of the people who have spoken, plus six others not present. You are replacing Professor Q. who is to retire shortly. Eventually you will replace your father. We thirteen are your father's advisors and only confidants. All other agents are misled as to the bulk of our objectives and motives. Their knowledge is restricted to the details required by their assignments. The penalty for disloyalty is death.

The Council is invaluable for propagating our policy decisions to our entourage without revealing our motives and strategy. In many instances, policy can he successfully sold to our entourage and thus transmitted to the multitudes by merely airing it along with appropriate rationalizations in a single awe-inspiring session of the Council. The informal power of the Council is such that our policy manipulations are usually attainable without the clumsy exercises in brute power that invariably snag the independent power seekers. The Council is at the heart of what is called the Establishment and we are at the heart of the Council.

At the Council's inception, we worked hard to attract the successful of all fields with all the prestige that our money power could buy. We had to work hard convincing the independent, self-made Council members to move in harmony with our policy objectives. We had many failures. Now everything is changed. Membership is no longer a reward for success as much as it is a prerequisite for major success. Without Council membership only the most outstanding can achieve national prominence. With membership, glaring mediocrities, with the "right" attitudes, achieve prominence. In fact, mediocrities are much more adapted to propagating our policy rationalizations and less likely to detect and oppose our ulterior motives. A power lusting mediocrity is not likely to judge his benefactors too harshly or inquire diligently into the nature of the power structure that brought him what he fears was undeserved success. The vanity of even idealistic, committed humanitarians militates against such a course.

The Council is now a giant employment agency of loyalists ready to parrot our public line from the commanding posts of government, foundations, broadcasting, industry, banking, and publishing. Although Council members are encouraged to take sides and bicker over the diversionary issues we create to entertain and enfeeble the populace, their solidarity in defending our power structure, root and branch, when pressed is a sight to behold! And to think that most see themselves as righteous defenders of the public good while they dismiss whispered rumors of our power structure as "kooky paranoia."

Classical secret societies with elaborate circles within circles no longer play a major role in finance capitalist power structures. Most wide membership secret societies have degenerated into middle class excuses for escaping the wife and kids once a month for the company of men. But secret societies were a major weapon of our bourgeoisie forebearers in their struggle with the old feudal order of kings and princes. Under authoritarian despotism of the old style, the secret society was the only place a free thinking man could express himself. Through threats of exposure, loyalty oaths, patronage, deception, and rewards we bound such malcontents into a fierce force for our revolution. The multitude of degrees, occult mumbo-jumbo, and vague humanitarianism concealed the real goals of our secret societies from the bulk of the membership. The roles of the "Illuminated" Masonic Lodges in European revolutions were decisive in our final victory over the old order.

I now yield the floor to Professor Y. who will discourse on the real "secret societies" the Modern Finance Capitalist State: the National Security Institutions and Intelligence Agencies.

8

"The 'covert' cloak of such above-ground operations is provided on the working assumption that the act can not be hidden, but that the onlooker's interpretation of its significance can be clouded by calculated misdirection."

—Lyndon LaRouche

"How can Mill fear that life will become uninteresting. To play on those millions of minds, to watch them slowly respond to an unseen stimulus, to guide their aspirations without their knowledge—all this whether in high capacities or in humble, is a big and endless game of chess, of ever extraordinary excitement."

—Sidney Webb, founder of the
Fabian Society, 1890

PROFESSOR Y. ON COVERT OPERATIONS AND INTELLIGENCE

In our fully developed state-capitalist systems we have found absolute control of governmental intelligence gathering and covert operations to be vital.

Besides providing a valuable tool in our struggle with rival dynasties, such control is now an integral and necessary part of our day to day operations. Large intelligence communities are inevitable, given the system of all encompassing governments which we have imposed upon the world during our ascent to power. Our power would be short-lived indeed if the pervasive influence and power of these iron-disciplined intelligence agencies fell into the hands of mere politicians, especially those beyond our control.

We do not allow intelligence agencies to pursue the "national interest," the way the public conceives "spies" to operate. Politicians cannot be permitted to divert the power and influence of our intelligence community from the esoteric requirements of our Money Power to petty political struggles.

Neither nationalistic aspirations of races and peoples nor ideological visions of intellectuals for humanity can be allowed to pervert intelligence and covert operations. Our rationalizations, both within the intelligence community and to the public at large, must be diverse and flexible, but the intelligence community must further without exception the inexorable goals we have set for humanity.

No crisis is more serious for our Money Power than an attempt by a head of government to assume personal control of intelligence and operations or to by-pass existing agencies by setting up parallel ones. Such intrusions must be met decisively. Although a contrived scandal to remove the offending politician from office is the first line of defense, we dare not shrink from assassination when necessary.

Perhaps the most accurate overview of our intelligence community can be achieved by visualizing it as a "nationalized secret society." Our predecessors, in their struggle against the old order of kings and princes, had to finance secret societies such as the Illuminati, Masons, German Union, etc. out of their own pockets. At great expense and risk such secret societies were able to infiltrate the major governmental and private institutions of the nations that our noble predecessors targeted for take over by the Money Power. Such bureaucratic take-overs are expensive and time consuming. They can be considered complete only when promotions, raises, and advancements are no longer based on objective service to the stated organizational objectives, but are in the hands of the infiltrating group and its secret goals.

How much easier it is for us, the inheritors of a fully developed state-capitalist system! By appealing to "national security" we are able to finance and erect secret societies of a colossal scope, far beyond the wildest dreams of our path breaking predecessors. Besides the benefits of public financing reaped by these "nationalized secret societies," we obtain a decisive advantage from the fact that these our "spook" operations are sanctioned by law!

Maintaining discipline, loyalty, and secrecy is no longer solely a matter of propaganda, blackmail, patronage, and intimidation. Although these remain important tools, especially in emergency cases, ordinary discipline among initiates (now called agents) can be encouraged by appealing to patriotism and can be enforced in courts of law by prosecuting "national security violations."

As massive as our intelligence community has become in itself, we still operate strictly on the finance capitalist principle of leverage. Just as a rational finance capitalist never owns more stock in a corporation than the bare minimum required for control, intelligence operatives are placed only in as many key positions as are required to control the target organizations. Our goal, after all, is agent control of all significant organizations, not intelligence community membership for the entire population.

The organizational pattern of baffling "circles within circles," characteristic of classical secret societies, is retained and refined by our intelligence community. That "one hand not know what the other is doing" is essential to the success of our operations. In most cases, we do not allow the operatives themselves to know the ultimate, and when possible, even the short-range objectives of their assignments.

They operate under "covers" that disguise our goals not only from the public and target groups, but from the agents themselves. For instance, many agents operating under "left cover" are led to believe that the agency, or at least their department, is secretly, but sincerely motivated by socialistic ideology. Thus, they assume that the intelligence agency's ultimate goal is to guide left-wing groups in "productive" directions, even though they cannot always see how their own assignment fits into those assumed goals.

Other "left-cover" agents, those with right-wing predilections, are encouraged to believe the agency is simply "monitoring" violence prone, subversive groups in order to protect the public. When such agents are asked to participate in or even lead radical activity they assume that the ultimate objective is to fully infiltrate and destroy the organization for the good of the country. This is very seldom the case. We waste little or no money protecting the "public" or defending the "nation."

Agents operating under "right-cover" are handled in symmetrical fashion. Agents with right-wing prejudices are encouraged to believe the agency is right-wing. Left-prejudiced agents are asked to operate under "right- cover" in order to "monitor" dangerous rightist organizations. Most intelligence agents remain blithely ignorant of the big picture which is so clear to us from our spectacular vantage point.

Very few have enough information or intelligence to reason out how their specific and sometimes baffling assignments promote the legislative, judicial, operational and propaganda needs of our Money Power. Most would never try. They are paid too much to think about such things.

Agents with a "gangster-cover" are of two types. First, there is the sincere gangster that draws his salary from an intelligence agency. He is led to believe that the gangland "Godfathers" control the government agency for their own purposes. Actually, the situation is the opposite. The agency controls the gangster for other purposes. Second, is the sincere crime fighter who is led to believe that the agency is attempting to infiltrate and monitor the gangsters as a preliminary step to destroying organized crime. Such "upstanding" agents commit many crimes in their zeal to rid the country of organized crime!

To envision how we operate in this lucrative field, let's briefly look at the mechanics of dope smuggling. Police and customs officials are told to leave certain gangsters alone, even when transporting suspicious cargo. This is made to seem perfectly proper since it is well known that secret police infiltrators of organized crime must participate in crimes in order to gain the confidence of gangsters.

What customs agent would want to upset a carefully laid plan to "set-up" the underworld kingpins of dope pushing! But the agent, as well as the police who cooperate, are mistaken in believing that the purpose of the assignment to help smuggle dope is ultimately to smash organized crime. If he could see the big picture, as we can, the agent would see that practically all our dope is smuggled by federal intelligence agents and secret police! How ever could such a volume be transported safely? Real harassment and prosecution is reserved for those who enter the field without our approval.

Here's our organized crime strategy: On the one hand we pass laws to ensure that mankind's favorite pastimes (vices) are illegal. On the other hand, we cater to these "vices" at a huge monopoly profit with complete immunity from prosecution.

A new and growing methodology of our intelligence community is psycho and drug-controlled agents. Properly, these are referred to as "behavior modified" agents, or, in the vernacular, "zombies." With the use of hypnotic drugs, brain washing, sensory deprivation, small group "sensitivity" training, and other behavior modification techniques, the scope of which was hinted in the movie *Clockwork Orange*, complete personalities can be manufactured from scratch, to the specifications of value structure profiles we design by computer to suit our purposes. Such personalities are quite neurotic and unstable due to defects in our still developing technology, but still useful for many purposes.

The primary virtue of "zombies," of course, is loyalty. Agents that are subconsciously programmed for the assignment at hand cannot be conscious traitors. All a "zombie" can do is reveal how compulsive and psychotic he is with regard to his "cause." Even to trained psychologists he simply appears to be the proverbial "lone nut." Although the "zombie" may have memories of psychotherapy at a government agency when questioned under hypnosis, this is unlikely to raise suspicion in the mind of court-appointed psychologists. After all, "lone nuts" should be kept in insane asylums and subjected to psychotherapy! At most, the government hospital will be reprimanded for letting a loony loose before he was cured.

Until our techniques can be perfected the use of "zombies" must be restricted to "national dramas" designed to justify the growing power of our centralized governments over the lives of our people. Most suicidal radicals and "crazies" who so mysteriously avoid arrest for years at a time are "zombies" conditioned to terrorize the public in the name of some irrational ideology. After repeated doses of such terror, the public is conditioned to accept the necessity of our intrusive police-state with very little objection.

The way is clear for an accelerated program of behavior

modification research to be conducted mostly at public expense in the name of mental health and rehabilitation. Such research can be conducted with little complaint in prisons, refugee camps, drug rehabilitation centers, government hospitals, veterans hospitals, and even public schools and day care centers. Mental institutions, methadone maintenance centers, and prisons are fertile fields for recruiting the deranged or drug addicted persons most suitable for "zombie" conversions. Of course, only a few of our most trusted agents actually participate in the creation of "zombies." The brilliant researchers and experimenters who make most of the break-throughs earnestly believe that their techniques are destined strictly for the betterment of mankind.

Inevitably, a fraction of the population objects to behavior modification as an infringement of man's "sacred" free-will even if they are convinced that our intentions are benign. We carefully leak a few scandals to satisfy such persons that our experiments are being kept within bounds and that excesses are being stopped. Our artificial scandals exposing the "excesses" of coercive psychology are carefully designed to make the researchers seem incompetent and clumsy to the point of maiming and killing their "patients." This effectively conceals the fantastic strides we have made toward total behavioral control. Great things are going to be possible in the future.

I now return the floor to your father for his concluding remarks.

"Might is a fine thing, and useful for many purposes; for one goes further with a handful of might than with a bagful of right."

—Max Stirner

"Why, then the world's mine oyster,
Which I with sword will open."

—Shakespeare

MY CLOSING REMARKS

MY SON, you surely have many questions about my strategy in the seemingly momentous economic and political crises that are shaking national and international affairs. You and I will begin handling them in detail shortly. For tonight, let me be brief. Most of the current national upheavals are stage-managed to consolidate our monopoly position in government and business against the continual nuisance of economically competent, but politically naive competitors. Likewise, most international crises are managed to exert pressure on our obstreperous, reluctant puppet dictators in underdeveloped areas. These events are fairly easy to manage. I expect to place such management in your hands as soon as possible.

The real challenge lies in dealing with my international peers. These are the real crises since they are crises of my power structure, not just of my subject populations and puppets. In the vast chess game with my peers there are no rules and no proven tactics. Mutual vulnerability, alone, limits the conflict. My peers and I have labored for decades to erect a world government and banking system under which we could all share finance capitalism's millennium without the nightmare of internecine warfare. With the advent of nuclear war a new world order seemed particularly desirable. I say ostensibly we have labored for world government because none of us are sure the others will ever voluntarily surrender sovereignty to the group. The schedule set after the last World War has not been met. So far, the world government idea has served mainly to enthuse collectivist intellectuals, and secondarily to veil each finance capitalist's maneuvers for supremacy from the rest.

The future course of finance capitalism is difficult to predict. Our empires are too fragile to risk all-out battles for supremacy among ourselves. Our power would dissipate to second echelon wealthy during the struggle. Yet we con-

tinue to chip away at rival empires on the premise that of-
fense is the best defense. On the other hand, purely political
leaders are helpless before our money power. When Caesars
arise, they are of our making.

Perhaps our system will simply remain much as it is, secure on the national level and disturbingly pluralistic at the
international level, until reason and egoism have developed
among our populations to such an extent that our occult
technology of money power becomes obvious to all who
think and must yield to either anarchy or a more advanced
form of deception

"The names of some of these banking families are familiar to all of us and should be more so. They include Baring, Lazard, Erlanger, Warburg, Schroder, Seligman, the Speyers, Mirabaud, Mallet, Fould, and above all Rothschild and Morgan."

—Dr. Carroll Quigley
Tragedy and Hope

AFTERWORD BY
THE TRANSCRIBER

Any resemblance of these characters to persons living or dead is purely coincidental. Any resemblance of their methodology to that of real ruling elites is purely intentional. The extent to which I represent or exaggerate the self-conscious, intentional power technology of real politico-economic rulers and their unity is for the reader to decide after studying available empirical evidence.

I am providing a bibliography of relevant historical works to aid the curious reader. I have included no works written from spurious pluralistic suppositions no one seems to consider pluralism as a proposition requiring evidence since they are flooding the market. Unfortunately, many works listed affirm that ideas rather than individual struggles for wealth and power propel history; that is, they view the elites they observe ruling the world as ideologically motivated. Thus we have the spectacle of the Right claiming that major finance capitalists such as the Rockefellers or Rothschilds are "communist" conspirators or "socialists." On the other hand, we see the Left claiming that the same people are bent on imposing *laissez-faire* capitalism, or in a slightly more realistic vein, are fanatical proponents of fascism. Virulent white racism is another ideology foolishly ascribed to the ruling class by the Left. This opinion is nicely balanced by the charge from the Right that the elite wants to "mongrelize" and thus submerge the white race. As usual the elite, completely free of prejudice, supports both sides of this battle for its own ends.

As should be clear by now, I believe that finance capitalists[6] are understandably attempting to make their power as extensive as possible without incurring the severe risks which

---

6   Ferdinand Lundberg has dubbed them *finpols*, or financial politicians

plague *pubpols* (public politicians).[7] *Pubpols* lose their privacy and thus their right to sexual impropriety in addition to incurring vulnerability to electioneering and worse in "democratic" countries. In most areas of the world the lot of the *pubpols* is even worse. Purge, assassination, and armed coup are regular events. While totalitarianism of Right or Left at home eliminates the shield of secure private property desired by *finpols*, *laissez-faire* is likewise rejected out-of-hand as hell-on-earth by enlightened power-seekers.

Egoism, mitigated only by the reality of circumstance, is the motive to realistically attribute to healthy elites. An elite under the spell of mental spooks could not hold sway for long. Although *finpol* statism is increasingly a crisis for its victims, there is as yet no evidence that the elite itself is in serious crisis. Even inflation, the current crisis for the powerless, is simply another crisis to be managed toward the end of consolidating, extending, and refreshing elite power. No doubt the depression which must inevitably follow will be managed to even better effect at the expense of the masses.

I have classified the bibliography into the categories Right and Left. In each list I begin with the most objective works and proceed to the works most infected with mental spooks and emotional hysteria. These books should be read for empirical data, not theoretical insight. A list of less ideologically biased works is provided as well. I quote and recommend authors, not to imply support for my scenario where there is none, but to credit a few of those who have provided grist for my thoughts.

---

7 It seems that only the most daring *finpols* are willing to take on the additional risks of *pubpoldom*, perhaps only because they are denied the reins to the family's fortune by more privileged relatives.

BIBLIOGRAPHY

"We are much beholden to Machiavelli and others, that
write what men do, and not what they ought to do."
—Francis Bacon

**INDISPENSABLE THOUGHTS ON HISTORY, ECONOMICS,
POLITICS, PHILOSOPHY, AND HUMAN NATURE.**

Murray N. Rothbard, *Economic Determinism and the Conspiracy Theory of History Revisited*, Audio-Forum. *America's Great Depression*, Nash, 1972.

Carroll Quigley, *The Evolution of Civilizations*.

Anton Szandor LaVey, *The Satanic Bible*, Avon Books, 1969.

Arkon Daraul, *Secret Societies*, Citadel Press, 1962.

Count Egon Caesar Corti, *The Rise of the House of Rothschild, The Reign of the House of Rothschild*, Cosmopolitan Book Corp., 1928.

Max Stirner, *The Ego and His Own*, Libertarian Book Club, 1963.

Robert Ardrey, *The Social Contract*, Dell Publishing, 1970.

Friedrich Nietzsche, *Beyond Good and Evil: Prelude to a Philosophy of the Future*, Random House, 1966.

George Orwell, *Animal Farm*, New American Library

Niccolo Machiavelli, *The Prince*, Encyclopedia Britannica, 1955.

Ludwig von Mises, *Theory and History*, Arlington House, 1969. *Human Action*, Henry Regnery, 1966.

James J. Martin, *Revisionist Viewpoints*, Ralph Myles Publisher, 1971.

Committee on Government Operations-U.S. Senate, *Disclosure of Corporate Ownership*, U.S. Government Printing Office, 1974.

Antony C. Sutton, *Wall Street and the Bolshevik Revolution, Wall Street and FDR*, Arlington House, 1975.

The Left on the Ruling Class

Carroll Quigley, *Tragedy and Hope*, Macmillan, 1966.

Gabriel Kolko, *The Triumph of Conservatism*, Quadrangle Books, 1967.

Richard Ney, *The Wall Street Gang*, Praeger Publishers, 1974.

Ferdinand Lundberg, *The Rich and the Super-Rich*, Lyle Stuart, 1968.
    America's 60 Families, Vanguard, 1938.

William G. Domhoff, *Who Rules America?* Prentice Hall, 1967. *The
    Higher Circles*. Random House, 1970.

Matthew Josephson, *Money Lords*, New American Library, 1973. *The
    Robber Barons*. Harcourt Brace & Co., 1934.

George H. Shibley, *The Money Question*, Stable Money Publishing
    Co., 1896.

Jules Archer, *The Plot to Seize the White House*, Hawthorn Books, 1973.

William Hoffman. *David: Report on a Rockefeller*, Dell Publishing,
    1972.

Joel Andreas, *The Incredible Rocky,* North American Congress on
    Latin America, 1973.

The Right on the Conspiracy Theory of History

Antony C. Sutton, *National Suicide*, Arlington House, 1973.

Charles A. Lindbergh, Sr., *The Economic Pinch*, Dorrance & Company, Inc., 1923, Reprinted by Omni Publications.

Louis T. McFadden, *Collective Speeches of Congressman McFadden*, Omni Publications, 1970.

H.S. Kenan, *The Federal Reserve Bank*, The Noontide Press, 1968.

Gary Allen, *None Dare Call It Conspiracy*, Concord Press, 1973. *Richard Nixon - The Man Behind the Mask*, Western Islands, 1971. *The Rockefeller File,* '76 Press, 1976.

Dan Smoot, *The Invisible Government*, The Dan Smoot Report, Inc., 1962.

W. Cleon Skousen, *The Naked Capitalist*, The Author, 1970.

Taylor Caldwell, *Captains and Kings,* Fawcett Publications, 1973.

John Robison, *Proofs of Conspiracy*, 1798, Reprinted by Western Islands.

Nesta Webster, *Secret Societies and Subversive Movements*, Christian Book Club, 1967.

A. N. Field, *The Truth About the Slump*, 1931, Reprinted by Omni Publications, 1962.

William Robert Plumme, *The Untold History*, The Committee for the Restoration of the Republic, 1964.

June Grem, *Karl Marx: Capitalist*, Enterprise Publications, 1972.

Emanuel Josephson, *Rockefeller Internationalist: Man Who Misrules the World*, Chedney Press, 1962.

APPENDIX

"A little gem of protocol which displays acute perception. A Satanic overview."

-Anton Szandor LaVey,
Cloven Hoof, Nov./Dec. 1974

THE OCCULT
TECHNOLOGY OF POWER

Reviewed by Joe Cobb, *Reason Magazine*, May, 1976

One of the most delightful little books of the last few years is either a satire or an updated version of Machiavelli's *Il Principe*. Written with a cynical, yet very clever statement of the techniques and methods with which "the father" has successfully consolidated and maintained a financial and political empire, the book presents a scenario which many readers will find persuasive. The fictional setting is given as the 30th birthday of "the son," heir-apparent to the reins of power. His father has gathered together seven close advisors at a weekend retreat to explain the family business, and

Alpine Enterprises Edition

to initiate "the son" into the brotherhood. The book is presented as the transcripts of that initiation.

The writer ("transcriber") comments: "Any resemblance of these characters to persons living or dead is purely coincidental. Any resemblance of their methodology to that of real ruling elites is purely intentional." This comment is in the last chapter, of course. In the first chapter he says: "My son, ... I have chosen you to be heir to my empire." Come all ye who lust after Power. Lick your chops-and read on!

Whether or not you accept the hypothesis of an international insiders' conspiracy, you must acknowledge the popularity of such an idea. The most eager supporters of conspiracy theories are young left-wing students and radical rightists. The U.S. Labor Party is very concerned about Nelson Rockefeller, only a heartbeat away from the Presidency. The Socialist Workers Party is positively convinced that giant corporations and finance capitalists rule the world. Anyone who puzzles over world affairs, and feels powerless to affect events, is susceptible to a conspiracy theory. *The Occult Technology of Power* should be a best seller among the Left. This reviewer would hope so, because the book is a good little primer on the economics of inflation and central banking. The writer argues in Chapter 2—entitled "On Occult Knowledge as the Key to Power"—that when secret magic tricks become public knowledge, the people become immune to mysticism and deception. The example of ancient astrology is interesting. The priests could use their mathematics and scrolls to predict the seasons. The common people, however, who based their planting and harvesting on the seasons could hardly even count to 21 (since few had six toes). The priests were able to sell their secret knowledge for wealth, power, and human sacrifices. Today, of course, astronomy is taught in grade schools and astrologers no longer frighten kings with their secret, occult powers.

Chapter 3 is entitled, "On the Economics of Central Banking." The writer points out that the common people no longer depend on the seasons, but the inflation and unemployment cycle is fearful and dangerous in a complex economic system. The little guy is afraid of losing his job, and the politician is afraid of protest at the polls. The modern occult "science" is economic prophecy.

Certainly the United States would have been spared a large measure of our current economic malaise if Nixon had not imposed wage-price controls in 1971. You will recall that at that time the pressure to "do something" about inflation, which had risen to 4.5 percent ("intolerable"), had become almost irresistible, and controls were very popular for a while. This is an example of modern mysticism, based on a massive public ignorance of economics. Who can doubt that if more people understood the sources of inflation, Congress would find itself eagerly slashing those so-called "uncontrollable" expenditures. Instead of demanding more credit expansion, the friends of the little guy might demand some price stability or deflation instead. The purpose of this book, aside from the author's profit motive (a noble purpose, to be sure), is summed up near the end by one of the young man's professors: "However, a trend toward rationality in human affairs plods along inexorably quite outside the reach of our power... Some have theorized that, eventually, widespread rational egoism will overturn our order." The little book is written as if it were a set of lectures by the central philosophers of a master conspiracy. Their personal viewpoint is rational egoism, but they want to keep the wisdom of this perspective secret-since it is impossible to exploit a person who maintains a self-conscious, self-interested frame of reference.

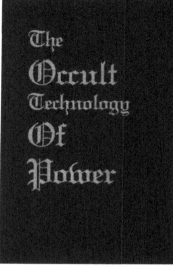

Loompanics Edition

By this time you have probably guessed that the writer, who remains anonymous as would befit an insider, is familiar with the writings of the libertarian philosophers. Insidiously, he counsels the young man, ". . . in the current era, while minds are yet in the thrall of altruistic, collectivistic, and divine moralistic spooks, the egoist's rational course is to utilize such spooks to control others." This is a very neat twist to the usual presentation libertarian writers make. It seems that Alpine Enterprises has given us a libertarian version of the Screwtape Letters.

This reviewer is very pleased with the discovery of a text we had at first avoided because of its title. The little book is very much worth its price. As Prof. Mises used to say, "Vote with your dollars." A vote of appreciation is in order.

You can find Mr. Cobb at www.JoeCobb.com

THE OCCULT
TECHNOLOGY OF POWER

Reviewed by Brian Wright, www.brianrwright.com, Oct. 2014

The Occult Technology of Power (*OTP*) is one of those sleeper-cell books, a book ahead of its time, more-or-less self-published by a disillusioned early Libertarian/libertarian activist. The author/publisher and I, with a handful of other young (it turns out naive) idealists, cofounded the Libertarian Party of Michigan, in June 1972 in Taylor, Michigan.

I say sleeper-cell because most in our milieu of those days were asleep when it came to understanding who actually stood behind the curtain of the Leviathan State. It didn't matter; we were going to crush the little commie pukes no matter what... and in record time. When *OTP* was issued, I think it meant something to about three **really radical** left-wing, hippie libertarians[1] living in a rundown flat somewhere in Long Beach, CA.

The movement I had entered was mainly of the right, initially Barry Goldwater libertarian-conservatism then leading through Ayn Rand rational-egoist individualism. We saw leftists as our supreme enemy, representing *in extremis* the Communist collectivist dictatorships of the time. By virtue of our own ideological alignment with private property and free enterprise we were largely oblivious to corporate-state corruption. Corporations were good guys in white hats, not evil beneficiaries of bonecrushing government franchise.

As arguments and protests emerged during the (60s and 70s) antiwar movement against the military-industrial complex and the ruling class, I admit to shamefully siding with what *actually composed* the police/corporate-state I

---

1   The prototype of libertarians receptive to the ruling-class-expose *OTP* message was Samuel Edward Konkin III (1947-2004), author of the *New Libertarian Manifesto* (1983) and founder of the Agorist Institute and the Movement of the Libertarian Left.

so loathed. Indeed, only relatively recently I understand how that state and its corporate and banking Mob have established frightening domination over the individual.

This little book, *OTP*, is probably the most succinct statement of who "they" are. Who rules, who pulls the strings, who picks the winners, who precipitates the wars, who commits the treachery... most important, who steals the wealth?!! The Transcriber locates the dead center of maximum political-economic sleaze in America and the world and delivers a smartbomb on target.

Noontide Press Edition

You read this book you understand the contrived conflict between right and left. You will know whose purposes it serves to have defenders of liberty hate those who question concentrations of power. As we fight among ourselves on higher-level issues—immigration, wars, terrorism, education, taxes, etc.—we leave the fundamental premise of state coercion intact... and make no mistake, the state we're talking about is the Cartel with a capital C.

You see the role of the government schools:

> A general state education is a mere contrivance for molding the people to be exactly like one another; and as the mold in which it casts them is that which pleases the predominant power in the government—whether this be a monarch, a priesthood, an aristocracy, or the majority of the existing generation—in proportion as it is efficient and successful, it establishes a despotism over the mind, leading by natural tendency to one over the body.
>
> —John Stuart Mill

You see the role of the central bank and taxes:

> As early as ancient Babylon and India, central banking, the art of monopolizing the issuance of money, had been developed into a perfect method for looting the general public. Even today many bankers copy the traditions of the earlier exploitative priesthoods and design their banks to resemble temples! Defenses of central banking are simply part of the deception that lies at the heart of all power elites.
>
> —*page 22*

The book conveys the instruction of a man in full, under auspices of his father, the leader of the Dynasty. (Speculation is the father-son pair is patterned after John D. Rockefeller, Jr. and David Rockefeller. Considering the Rockefeller family through banking, business, foundations, and other holdings controls trillions of dollars in human wealth, the pattern is apt.)

The father introduces his soon-to-be Supreme Financial Politician (finpol) successor to the mysteries of how the Dynasty—by the way, the Rockefeller dynasty is the predominant component in what I typically call the Cartel, or sometimes the Beast or the Empire—exercises its nearly complete control of society.

It's a quick read, showing astonishing and timely insight into the Big Universal Problem (BUP) that ails us. I wish the Transcriber had covered the income tax a bit more thoroughly and that he would have elaborated on the controlled-media propaganda machinery. Quibbles.[2]

As honest journalists and "causality theorists," we cannot close the book on further inquiry... that may augment or even contradict an earlier consensus. That said, *Occult* is a book that demands to be resurrected and handed out to your friends and acquaintances in all walks of life. We've

---

2   On a personal note, in current times (2010+) my understanding of the corporotocracy/toxocracy has taken a turn toward the view of the Thrive movement, et al, which has elicited more than a few contrary emotional reactions on my site from Mr. Transcriber. We both live in the greater Detroit area.

reached a point where increasing numbers of real people intuitively realize what's going on; *OTP* will cement that knowledge.

Interestingly, the Ron Paul Nation phenomenon is a direct result of people being "mad as hell and not about to take it any more." Dr. Paul is a strong advocate of schools freed from state compulsion and a firm opponent of the Federal Reserve System and its corollary interest-earning tool, the income tax. It is not difficult to see why the Cartel politicians and media are excreting Frisbees for fear the RP message may catch on: they'll all wind up in the dustbin of history along with Divine Kings.

A Publication of
Alpine Enterprises
Volume I, No. 1

THE Conspiriologist

AN ACCESS CATALOG FOR ADVANCED STUDENTS OF CONSPIRACY THEORIES.

CONSPIRACY DIGEST

IN THIRD YEAR
OF PATHBREAKING
PUBLICATION!

Alpine Enterprises Announces:
NEW POLICY ON RARE BOOKS

The rapidly growing interest in ruling class/ conspiracy theories in Right, Left, and Libertarian political circles has created explosive demand for the rare, hard-to-find, and out-of-print classics in the field. While this brisk demand has enabled *Alpine Enterprises* to remain in business during a time when the mail order industry is being laid low by absurd postal rate hikes, problems have also been created. Many books that we used to supply routinely for less than $10.00 now command prices from $20.00-$50.00 and require an unpredictable wait. It has become impossible to stock at preset prices many of the books we used to carry.

This new situation has forced us to create a new policy as follows:

1. Only the books advertised at set prices in the *Conspiriologist* are stocked for immediate shipment. Only these books can be ordered with confidence of immediate shipment and price stability.

2. For our full list of books, you should order a back issue of our previous tabloid catalog: *The Suppressed Truth Review*. While prices are often out-of-date, you will find the book descriptions extremely valuable.

3. Books not listed in the *Conspiriologist* but listed in the *Suppressed Truth Review* may be purchased on an inquiry basis only. Just send in a list of the books you

OCCULT TECHNOLOGY OF POWER PUBLISHED IN HARDCOVER

Alpine Enterprises grew out of an unexpected response to its vanity publication in 1974 of a strange book titled *The Occult Technology of Power (OTP)*. While initial response was slow due to confusion concerning the word "Occult," which was used in the pristine sense of "hidden" rather than the vulgar sense of "mystical," word of mouth promotion soon led to a steady stream of urgent letters requesting information on how to obtain the rare books in *OTP's* bibliography.

The *Occult Technology of Power* is a masterpiece in a class of its own. Written from the point-of-view of master conspirators instructing one of their own of the intricacies of their power and statist-economic manipulations, *OTP* is a powerful force in bringing the day that such conspiracy becomes impossible and a subject of historical interest only.

OTP has an uncanny ability to make scornful doubters take a second look, and then, an about face. Apparently, evil is so foreign to decent folk that only a first person narrative is capable of breaking through the fallacy of projecting "good intentions."

Joly's *Dialogues in Hell Between Machiavelli and Montesquieu* captured something of the same magic. In fact, the magic was so strong that the Czar's totalitarians plagiarized it and perverted it into an anti-Semitic diatribe that has since been used as propaganda to prop up tyranny by Hitler and Nasser. Fortunately, *OTP's* message is thoroughly pro-liberty, anti-State, and cannot be perverted to serve State tyranny as was the earlier Joly work.

The *Occult Technology of Power* is must reading for anyone who enjoys an intellectual challenge.

"AVAILABLE AS FREE GIFT WITH CONSPIRACY DIGEST SUBSCRIPTION"

CONSPIRACY DIGEST SUBSCRIPTIONS:
NOW A BARGAIN YOU CAN'T REFUSE!

At the same time we find it nearly impossible to keep up with the orders from advanced students for rare and

are offering these books as inducements for *Conspiracy Digest* subscribers. By this approach we hope to

CONSPIRACY VS. LIBERTY

WHY PROPONENTS OF LIBERTY MUST NOT IGNORE CONSPIRACY

Unless a computer list mistake has occurred, I would be wasting ink arguing to you that economic, political, and personal liberties have suffered severe blows from big government in America, to say nothing of in the rest of the world. (You already agree.)

The question is, *Why?* If liberty is so demonstrably beneficial to the vast majority of the people, both for their physical and spiritual well-being, why are the people so opposed to it? Everyone who is interested in this question has their favorite answer: laziness, greed, subjectivity, genetic deterioration, complexity of technology, alienation, low I.Q., innate envy, the nuclear family, the break-down of the nuclear family, religion, the lack of religion, rationality, lack of reason, faith, lack of faith, etc., etc.

While all these factors and more may contribute to making a particular individual more likely to reject liberty in favor of big government dependence, we do not believe that they are *causal* factors.

A primary datum to be considered is the division of labor. To master the pros and cons of liberty, especially in economics, a great deal of time, effort, and reading is required. Thus, the vast majority of people simply *can-not* decide these issues through first-hand analysis.

The next obvious question is *who* does their thinking for them? True, a few intellectuals like Ludwig von Mises, Murray Rothbard, Ayn Rand, von Hayek, Milton Friedman, etc., attempt and succeed to an extent in making their living presenting the case for liberty in an organized form that segments of busy humanity will hopefully have time to study.

As everyone knows, their voices are drowned out by the advocates of tyranny. Why? Milton Friedman has

suggested that there is a *demand* for economic nonsense and unprincipled intellectuals simply respond to that "free market" demand for nonsense. We believe that this view is more than paradoxical. It is incorrect.

We believe that the economic nonsense which rationalizes tyrannous big government is subsidized to the extent required to keep such opinions dominant in the culture by the vested interests which profit from government control. For now, we can leave open the question as to whether these vested interests form a monolithic, interlocking network that culminates in the authority of David Rockefeller as Chairman of the Chase Manhattan and the Council on Foreign Relations (or Lords Rothschild, Royal Institute?) In any case, we do not believe that it is a coincidence that government control systematically achieves the opposite of the alleged "egalitarian" intent.

While it may not be obvious at first, the above insight will accomplish a revolution of educational tactics in the movement for liberty. The task of converting humanity into billions of economic experts will finally be recognized futile and laughably hopeless. Instead, educational efforts can be directed toward the real (but admittedly not simple) task of exposing the real enemies of mankind — the powers behind the state — the profiteers of government coercion. In this happy task the movement for liberty shall have the powerful forces of envy and resentment on their side for a change! And the "envy" so mobilized to destroy government tyranny will be the rational, justified envy (would outrage be a better word?) of the oppressed against real oppressors!

Believe it or not, victory for liberty could be closer than you think!

"CONSPIRACY EXPOSÉ IS THE MOST EFFECTIVE WAY TO FIGHT AGAINST BIG GOVERNMENT TYRANNY AND FOR INDIVIDUAL LIBERTY"

classifieds

Classified ad from Reason Magazine, *January, 1975*